D0940994

The Turn of the Years

The Turn of the Years

The Seasons' Course
SELECTED ENGRAVINGS BY
REYNOLDS STONE

As Old as the Century
V. S. PRITCHETT

WITH AN INTRODUCTION BY
PAUL THEROUX

RANDOM HOUSE
NEW YORK

All rights reserved under International
and Pan-American Copyright Conventions.
Published in the United States by Random House, Inc.,
New York and simultaneously in Canada by
Random House of Canada Limited, Toronto.
Published in Great Britain by
Michael Russell (Publishing) Ltd.,
The Chantry, Wilton, Salisbury, Wiltshire.

Introduction © 1982 Paul Theroux
Wood engravings © 1982 Janet Stone
(and see Acknowledgements, p. 48)
'As Old as the Century' by V. S. Pritchett was published
(under the title 'Looking Back at Eighty')
in the December 14, 1980, issue of
The New York Times Magazine.
© 1980 by The New York Times Company.
Reprinted by permission.
'As Old as the Century' was also published in *The Observer*.

Library of Congress Cataloging in Publication Data

Pritchett, V. S. (Victor Sawdon), 1900–
The turn of the years.

1. Pritchett, V. S. (Victor Sawdon), 1900–
—Biography. 2. Authors, English—20th century—
Biography. I. Title
PR6031.R7Z47   828'.91203 [B]   81-48494
ISBN 0-394-52502-7   AACR2
ISBN 0-394-52501-9 (deluxe)

Designed by Humphrey Stone

Set in Monophoto Ehrhardt
Printed and bound in Great Britain

98765432

FIRST AMERICAN EDITION

Contents

Introduction

This book came about through luck, friendship and coincidence. V. S. Pritchett wrote a reflective essay last year for his eightieth birthday. It appeared in a Sunday newspaper. It seemed to me wise and funny; it was beautifully written—a summing up, lit with great happiness. It deserved more permanent record, but Pritchett had no immediate plans to include it in a collection. 'Why not make a small book of it?' I said. 'By all means,' Pritchett said. Michael Russell agreed—and he was at that moment sorting through some Reynolds Stone wood engravings.

The Pritchetts and the Stones first met in 1950. Their houses were in neighbouring villages in Berkshire. They were soon close friends, they exchanged visits, and then, in time, they moved—the Stones to the Dorset village of Litton Cheney, the Pritchetts to London. Reynolds Stone hated London. Pritchett says, 'He was an open-air man.' After that, the Pritchetts—Victor and Dorothy—visited Reynolds and Janet Stone in the country.

'Reynolds was an extraordinary man.' Pritchett glanced at the Reynolds Stone watercolour as he spoke. The picture, of undergrowth and pale damp woods, was entirely green. 'He saw himself as a Victorian figure—and he was. He loved listening. He didn't talk a great deal. He had a very remarkable appearance, very slender, with striking eyes. He looked at times almost Chinese. He loved detail. The details of buildings—that gutter, that turret. You can see that in his engravings. And there was a touch of the pedant about him. He liked local knowledge, and craftsmen. He could have told you where to find a wheelwright. This love of detail was also a kind of patience. When his mail came he would pick up the envelopes, turn them over, examine the stamps, peer closely at them, and put them down without opening them.

'Reynolds and Janet were excellent hosts in the old style. You had a coal fire in the bedroom. Dinner parties, organised activities, people dropped in. And there was an uncle about with an enormous number of gramophone records in the barn. Reynolds sat and worked with the room full of people. There he was, engraving and listening. He loved company, even when he was working.'

Reynolds Stone, who died in 1979, was nine years younger than V. S. Pritchett. Stone, the artist, had a fine library; Pritchett, the writer, often sketched and painted, privately. But Stone did not talk much about his reading, and Pritchett never revealed that he drew pictures for pleasure.

There were close similarities in their visions of the world. Both men are compassionate; there is conviction in their work. It is not surprising that they were friends, or that this book of pictures and print strikes such a lovely balance, which is fearless and bright. Both men show in their art how time passes, and how the movement of time changes us and makes us live, if we are fully awake.

November 1981   PAUL THEROUX

Or where I found thy yellow bed
Below the hill-borne fir-tree's head,
And heard the whistling east wind blow
Above, while wood-screen'd down below
I rambled in the spring-day's glow,
And watch'd the low-ear'd hares upspring
From cover, and the birds take wing.
  Come, winter moss, creep on, creep on,
  And warn me of the time that's gone.

from 'Moss' by William Barnes

As Old as the Century

As Old as the Century

V. S. PRITCHETT
AT EIGHTY

Since my boyhood I have been vain of being born just before the end of 1900 and at every birthday thinking of myself as pretty well as old as the century. I was at ease with its assumptions for fourteen years: after that, two dreadful wars, huge social changes, technological revolution, the disappearance of British power, the rise of the Welfare State, a decade or two of 'peace' in the world abroad, dramatic threats once more.

Now I am eighty I see I have been shaken up like a dice in a box, if not as brutally as people born ten years earlier than myself. Many are still alive and in voice. I am abashed by my survival rather than proud of it; there is no merit in it. The credit goes to those secretive gamblers we call the genes.

I come of long-lived forebears among whom there were few defaulters on the Yorkshire side. Also, because of the great advances of medical science and hygiene, the average expectation of life in Great Britain has enormously increased in the past fifty years or more. The old are no longer revered curiosities; on the contrary, often a social problem. We swarm in cities and resorts, ancient mariners who square our shoulders as we pick one another out at a glance in the pubs, the shops, the park seats, the planes and the tourist buses. Our skins do not yet give off the eerie smell of senility. That glance of ours is often frisky, conspiratorial and threatening, warning you that we could a tale unfold if we should happen to get a grip on your wrist.

Not a day's illness—we boast—except a winter cough or a twinge of arthritis or gout; we speak of these twitches as medals we have won. Smoke like fish (we go on), drink like a chimney, pity people who do not work a twelve-hour day, who have not ducked their heads through two world wars or known the good old hard times. And as for this new thing called sex . . !

As our tongues wag and our metaphors mix we turn into actors on our conspicuous stage. We are good at pretending to be modest; we refuse to acknowledge we are ever in the wrong or incompetent. A brisk eighty-year-old electrician came to do a job at my house six years ago and serenely drove his drill clean through a hidden water pipe I had warned him of. He turned accusingly on me as the water

[32]

spouted over us. Like all us oldies he congratulated himself and boasted he had never done such a thing to a water pipe. He and I still greet each other as we rush by in the street, equals in conceit and folly, and say how young we feel.

Our acting is, of course, a defence against our fear of senility and death. What shall we be like in our nineties? Are we for the old folks' home? We have seen so many of our friends paralysed, collapsing in mind and physically humiliated. Shall we escape? Yet, behind our acting there is also the knowledge that age does not march mathematically year by year with the calendar. One's real age stands still for large blocks of time.

My hair is now white and veins stand out on my temples, I have dark brown spots on my hands, my arms shrink, but to my mind I seem to be much what I was at fifty: at fifty-seven I looked despairingly bleak, ill and flaccid, to judge from a photograph, less brisk than I became in my sixties, seventies or today. Middle age was more agonising and trying than the later years have been, but perhaps my age has always gone up and down because I am one of those who 'live on their nerves'. I know one thing for certain: I was far, far younger in my thirties than I had been in my twenties, because my heart was fuller at thirty, my energies knew their direction, chiefly due to a happy marriage. It has lasted forty-four years. There is nothing like a *coup de foudre* and absorption in family responsibility for maturing the male and pulling his scattered wits together. I became physically stronger after years of bad health. Yet I had not lost what I valued in my twenties: living for the liberation of the moment.

Today I still go fast up the four flights of steep stairs to my study in our tall late-Nash house, every day of the week, at nine o'clock in the morning, Saturdays and Sundays included, cursing the Inland Revenue and inflation, groaning at the work I have to do, crying out dishonestly for leisure, thinking of this year's holiday and the ten-mile walks on the cliffs of North Cornwall, complaining that surely at my age I should be able to get some time off.

Why, even when I travel, do I still have to work? But the moment I've cleaned my pipe and put pen to paper the groans stop. I am under the spell of language which has ruled me since I was ten. A few minutes later—four hours' writing have washed out all sense of time—my wife calls me down to a delicious lunch. She has spent the morning typing what I wrote the day before, laughing at my bad spelling, inserting sportive words when she can't read my insectile hand—that has got smaller—and knowing she'll have to do the whole damn thing over again two or three times because I cover each page with an ant's colony of corrections; she is a perfectionist too.

[34]

We enjoy working together; she has a better memory than I have and I depend on her criticism. It is she who charms away the swarms of people who telephone, the speculators who think I exist for reading their theses and books, for more and more reviews, for giving interviews or lectures or signing their applications for grants. She has also driven off the droppers-in, the Mormons and Jehovah's Witnesses and other enemies of a writer's life. She is much younger and more decisive than I am.

After lunch I have a nap for an hour, do some household shopping in Camden Town where I pass as an old pensioner called Pritchard—very suited to a writer's double life—and return to take up tea and then back to work about four until seven and then a couple of Martinis, eat, try to catch up with letters and bills or in good weather go out and work in the garden. Unless we are going out we are in bed by ten. I sleep pretty well, dream wildly; the bad nights are those when I go on writing in my sleep, in English mostly but often, out of vanity, in Spanish, French or in dog-German which I stopped learning when I left school at fifteen. For Latin I have to rely on my wife.

I am a very lucky man, of course. If our pleasant house among the old trees of the quiet terrace is too large for us now our family have grown up, after twenty-five years here where else could we go with thousands of books? Would that frozen Buddha—the freezer that has changed our lives—fit in a new kitchen? Moving would betray our furniture and new draughts often kill old men.

I am lucky to be able to work at home, to commute upstairs instead of by train or bus. It is lucky I am still able to earn my living as a writer which I dreamed of when I was a boy. Thomas Hardy, in his old age, told Virginia Woolf that to write poetry was simply a matter of physical strength. So is writing prose. And that energy I was given by my parents: my Kentish Town mother's energy was nervous, my father's had the obdurate Yorkshire self-will. I cannot claim credit as an heir to this enlivening mixture of fortune which has generated in me a mixture of fantasy and wry common sense.

I am fortunate in these times which are hard for many workers—especially the pensioned-off or redundant—to be 'in work'. Many a pensioner, forced to be idle against his will, has greater reserves of character than I have. I do have my occasional days of leisure, but for the most part I have to carry what Keats called the indispensable sense of 'negative capability' about with me and then, as he also said, work makes 'the disagreeables evaporate'.

I look back now at my 'evaporations' with astonishment. If I spent my boyhood in the low Kippsian regions of Edwardian Britain, the British assurance and locality had given an elegance to British comedy.

The 'man of letters' I aspired to be was pre-eminent, if poor, in English periodical writing. Also modest families like mine were beneficiaries of the Education Act of the 1870s. Disagreeable to have education cut short at fifteen, but there had been a brief evaporation into foreign languages at a grammar school, language of any kind being my obsession.

It was disagreeable at first to be put into the malodorous leather trade, but the animality of skins fascinated me and so did the Bermondsey leather dressers and fellmongers. The smell of that London of my boyhood and bowler-hatted youth is still with me. I coughed my way through a city stinking, rather excitingly, of coal smoke, gas escapes, tanyards, breweries, horse manure and urine. Flies swarmed, people scratched their fleas. The streets smelled of beer; men and boys reeked of hair oil, vaseline, strong tobacco, powerful boot polish, mackintoshes and things like my father's voluptuous cachous.

The smell of women was racy and scented. Clothes were heavy; utterances—in all classes—were sententious whether witty or not. Music hall songs were epigrammatic stories. 'Lurve' had not yet killed them. Artful euphemism hid a secret archive of bad language. If a 'bloody' broke through, people would say 'Language, I hear,' disapproving as they admired. Hypocrisy was a native fruit, if then overripe.

By 1918 the skirts of the liberated girls who had

worked in ammunition factories and offices were shortened a few inches. One now saw their erotic ankles and sex broke out; not as yet in plain Anglo-Saxon, but soon Latinised as copulation in the classier Twenties, for youths like myself who had moved on to Aldous Huxley. I had read enormously, most of Scott, Dickens, most of the Victorian novelists, caught up with Chesterton and Bennett and was heading for *Anna Karenina* and *Madame Bovary*.

I might have stuck in leather all my life but 1918 liberated me. Travel was cheap; I 'evaporated' to Paris, earned my living in the shellac and glue trade and discovered I could write sketches. I became the autodidact abroad and education was open to me at last.

It was even good luck to grow up among non-intellectual people, all in trades; better luck, to have a vocation fixed in my mind—so few boys have—to grow up in a period when the printed language was the dominant teacher and pleasure-giver. Good luck to escape, by going abroad, the perpetual British 'no' to the new boy; good luck to meet the American 'yes' to my first bits of writing. France, Ireland, Spain were for six years my universities. They taught me European history and the conflicts of cultures and quickly got me clear of the hurdles of the then sticky English class system. Once they have made their bid, all kinds of artists—writers, painters, sculptors,

[38]

musicians, educated or not—are free of that. It is also half-native in our tribe that we can talk and listen to anyone in his language. Among writers Kipling is an exemplar of what travel does for this faculty.

Since the wilful Twenties, the committals of the Thirties, it seems to me that my life as a man and as a writer has been spent on crossing and recrossing frontiers and that is at the heart of any talent I have. It cheers me that I live on the frontier of Camden Town and Regent's Park. Frontier life has been nourishing to me. Throwing something of oneself away is a way of becoming, for the moment, other people, and I have always thought that unselfing oneself, speaking for others, justifying those who cannot speak, giving importance to the fact that they live, is especially the privilege of the storyteller, and even the critic—who is also an artist.

And here, at the age of forty when the Second World War seemed that it would ruin my life as a short story writer, novelist and critic, I found that my early life in trade was an advantage: it prepared me for another evaporation. I had to divide my time between serious criticism in the *New Statesman* every week and studies of factories, mines, shipyards, railway sidings and industrial towns. I did my literary work in trains. I have always been wary of what used to be called 'committal' to the social and political ideologies which numbers of my contemporaries preached and now in war my foreignness abated: I began to know once more how my own people lived: that abstraction called The People dissolved as I saw real people living lives in conditions unlike my own but with passions like mine and as proud of something unique in them.

The decisive books of the period about English life for me were Jack Common's *The Freedom of the Streets* and—on the Spanish war—Borkenau's *The Spanish Cockpit*. I found my own *raison d'être* in some words of Dostoevsky's that 'without art a man might find his life on earth unliveable'.

If as a storyteller I have had an ear for how people speak and my travelling, bookish nature turned me into that now fading type, a man of letters, how do I see the changes that have slowly come about in the past forty years? In a searching way these changes were predicted in the late Thirties by Louis Mumford in his absorbing book *The Culture of Cities*. My London has become a megalopolis. It has turned into a fantastic foreign bazaar. The Third World is replacing the traditional European immigrants.

Mumford argued that social betterment has been outstripped every decade by technology. We have become, or feel we have become, anonymous items in a mass society at once neutral and bizarre. As for technology the printed word no longer predominates in popular taste and, as Auden said, literature is now turning into 'a cottage industry'. The descendants of ordinary people who read their Dickens and the Victorian and Edwardian periodicals have given up the printed word for the instant sensation of sight and sound, for pictures on the screen.

One can tell this, if by nothing else, from popular speech in which half the vowels and consonants are missing, and in which a sentence becomes like one slurred word, a telegraphic message. The schools have turned out a large number of grown men and women who cannot read or write, for machines have made this unnecessary for them. I suppose the small core of addicted readers will remain, just as Latin remained for the medieval clerks, but the outlook for prose is not good. The new generation faces the attack of spoken and visual drama which cuts out our prose.

No professional writer becomes famous until his work has been televised or filmed: the rest of us may have to live in the conceit of being like the lamenting figures in the chorus of the Greek drama. That chorus was, in its tedious, humble way, the indispensable gang of prosing human moralists chanting the general dismay as they watched the impersonal and violent passions murderously at work on a stage without backcloth. We may of course become Aristophanic fabulists mocking the ruling cliques of a State Machine. Anthony Burgess and Angus Wilson are revelling in this at the moment.

There is another danger to literary culture: it comes from the technological habits of academic criticism. Scholars have been for ages the traditional conservers of literary tradition, but under the powerful influences of technology and the sciences, linguistics, psychology, sociology, philosophy, they are now using a new and portentous verbiage. They detach themselves from life and reduce it to an esoteric game or treat it as a kind of engineering. Their commentaries are full of self-important and comic irrelevancies. Their specialised ironmongery may be good training for engineers, scientists and spacemen, but it has little relation to imaginative literature.

I speak from experience for—to my astonishment as one who had never been inside any university until I was turned fifty—I have found myself teaching at Princeton, Berkeley, Columbia and the delightful Smith College, in the United States. I suppose to give their tormented Faculties a rest while I unloaded a chattering mind that has always read for delight. I like teaching because it wakes me up and teaches *me* and I am grateful to those institutions for giving me the free time an imaginative writer needs and which I get little of in England.

From my earliest days I have liked the natural readiness and openness of the American temperament and I had been brought up in childhood a good deal on the classic American writers and their direct response to the world they lived in. If American seriousness is often exhausting, the spontaneous image-making vernacular and wit are excellent. American short stories have often an archaic directness more striking than our own. I must also say that some of the most illuminating and helpful remarks about my own writing have come from American critics who, unlike so many of our own, are not out to display themselves rather than the authors they are dealing with. As for the American student—naive and earnest he may sometimes be, as I was when young; but he is continuously expectant and is without the European sneer.

At eighty I look at the horrible state of our civilisation. It seems to be breaking up and returning to the bloody world of Shakespeare's Histories which we thought we had outgrown. But public, like private life, proceeds in circles. The Third World is reliving history we have forgotten and indeed brings its violence to our cities. I am a humanist but I do not think human beings are rational: their greeds and passions are not quickly outgrown. We have now to school ourselves to deal with danger and tragedy.

I have some stoicism but I have often thought lately of a courageous friend of mine, now dead, an adventurous explorer, mountaineer and rather reckless yachtsman. He was one of those born to test his fears. I once sailed in a wild gale with him—much against my will—and was terrified, for I am afraid of the sea and have never learned to swim more than ten yards. He was not afraid. Or, if he feared, his fears exhilarated him and, in fact, vanished in danger because (he said) he was always 'thinking of the next thing to do'. (I suppose this is what I do, when I leave land for the perils of writing prose in which there have been so many shipwrecks.) In physical danger I am capable only of identifying myself with my evil: not as good a recourse as his, but it helps.

I have another friend, eighty-six years old, who has lately been hit by a tragedy in his family. He said he wanted to die at once—but not, he added, until he had seen what happened next in Poland and after that in Iran. At eighty I find myself on the lookout expectantly for the unexpected and am more than half allured by it.

Am I wiser in my old age? I don't know. I am not yet old enough to know loneliness and that puts one to the tests of folly and rage. But I am more tolerant than when I was young. I was not an affectionate young man and indeed I was thought of as fierce—a bolting pony, someone once said. But passionate love made me affectionate. I am deeply touched by the affection I now receive. It is one of the rewards of old age. I suppose I am slowly growing up. I am not a man's man for I owe much to women since my boyhood when my mother fascinated me by the whirligig of her humour and her emotions. And what about serenity? I see that many old women have it. In men it is more often torpor and I am drawn to activity and using myself. And to laughter, which wakes up the mind.

Strangely, laughter seems to me like the sexual act which is perhaps the laughter of two bodies. Whatever there is to be said for serenity there is not much opportunity for it in the modern world; and indeed I know by watching myself that old people are liable to fantasies of sadistic vengeance. The old should not look at the news on television at night.

The pleasures of old age are of the lingering kind, love itself becomes more mysterious, tender and lasting. The great distress of old age is the death of friends, the thinning ranks of one's generation. The air grows cold in the gaps. Something of oneself is drained away when friends go, though in mourning for them we learn to revalue a past we had more than half forgotten, and to bring them walking back to keener life in our memory. We have been members of one another. In old age we increasingly feel we are strangers and we warm to those who treat us as if we are not.

The new sensation is that living people are a wonder. Have you noticed how old people stare at groups of talkers, as if secretly or discreetly joining them silently at a distance? This does not happen to me much for I am always on the move, but I am aware of it. I used to sit long over my beer in pubs and clubs; now I swallow a double gin and run. I don't know why. Trying to pack more into the day? No: I just want to get home.

A sign of old age in myself is that, knowing my time is limited, I find myself looking at streets and their architecture much longer and more intensely and at Nature and landscape. I gaze at the plane tree at the end of the garden, studying its branches and its leaves. I look a long time at flowers. And I am always on the watch for the dramatic changes in the London sky. I have always liked to sketch formations of clouds. I store up the procession of headlands and terrifying ravines of North Cornwall and of all the landscapes that have formed me: the shapes of the Yorkshire Fells and the Downs in Sussex and Wilt-shire, the tableland of Castile.

I have no religious faith. I am no pantheist or sentimentalist in my love of Nature but simply an idolater of leaf, hill, stream and stone. I came across a line of Camus which drily describes people like myself:

'One of our contemporaries is cured of his torment simply by contemplating a landscape.'

That, and lately falling into the habit of reading

Gibbon's *Decline and Fall* on Sunday evenings, 'evaporates the disagreeables' of history that now advance on us: the irony of the learned Gibbon excites the sense of tragi-comedy and is, except for its lack of poetic sense, close to the feeling I have about the present and the past.

Acknowledgements

The engravings on pp. 9 and 19 and versions of the engravings on p. 12 (above) and p. 23 (below) appeared in *The Open Air* by Adrian Bell, Faber & Faber, 1949; p. 12 (below) — *The Skylark and Other Poems* by Ralph Hodgson, Colin Fenton (distributed by Rupert Hart-Davis), 1958; pp. 13, 18, 26, 28 (above) — Oxford University Press quarterly list, 1959; p. 14 — title page design for *Ambush of Young Days* by Alison Uttley, Faber & Faber, 1937; pp. 17, 22 (above), 25 (below) — *The Praise and Happinesse of the Countrie-Life* by Don Antonio de Guevara, trans. H. Vaughan, Gregynog Press, 1938; pp. 23, 27 — *Tit for Tat*, collection of songs by Benjamin Britten, Faber Music, 1969; p. 24 — *Old English Wines and Cordials* by T. Read, comp. J. E. Masters. High House Press, 1938; p. 25 (above) — jacket design for first edition of *The Open Air* by Adrian Bell, Faber & Faber, 1936; frontispiece — *The Old Rectory* series, Warren Editions, 1976. We acknowledge with thanks the cooperation of John Murray (Publishers) Ltd., publishers of *Reynolds Stone Engravings* (1977).